Original title:
Golden Sands, Blue Oceans

Copyright © 2025 Creative Arts Management OÜ
All rights reserved.

Author: Lucas Harrington
ISBN HARDBACK: 978-1-80581-595-2
ISBN PAPERBACK: 978-1-80581-122-0
ISBN EBOOK: 978-1-80581-595-2

Vitreous Shores Beneath the Sun

With flip-flops on, we run amok,
The seagulls squawk, they think they're rock.
We chase the waves, they splash our feet,
Life's a circus, oh what a treat!

Sunburnt noses, laughter loud,
A beach ball lands, it draws a crowd.
We build a castle, it lasts a breeze,
Then watch it fall—oh, such a tease!

Iridescent Shores of Reflection

With sunscreen smeared, we look quite grand,
A group of clowns upon the sand.
We search for crabs, they scuttle fast,
We try to catch them, but fail—at last!

A sunhat flies, oh what a show,
It sails away, we watch in woe.
We laugh so hard, our bellies ache,
This beach day joy, no heart can break!

A Maze of Light and Water

A beach umbrella tilts with might,
And soon becomes a party site.
We sip on drinks, our straws go wild,
The ocean's waves, our splashy child!

The tide rolls in, we squeal in glee,
As jellyfish dance, as brave as we!
We dodge the surf and play like fools,
The salty breeze, our swimsuits' jewels!

Serenity in the Salt-Kissed Breeze

With buckets high, we dig for treasure,
The sand's our canvas, oh what pleasure!
But finding gold? That's quite a task,
We settle for shells, oh what a blast!

The sun sets low, a wobbly kite,
We cheer it on, just like a fight.
With belly laughs and giggles sweet,
Our salty memories, none can beat!

Celestial Waves and Sunlit Paths

On shores so bright, seagulls squawk,
My sunhat flies with each silly walk.
Waves crash in joy, tickling my toes,
Watch out for crabs, or they'll strike a pose!

Sandcastles rise, but oh, what a flop,
My little brother makes them go plop.
We laugh as the tide takes our work away,
Building again, it's a whole new play!

Sun-Drenched Footprints

Footprints dance on the warm, soft grain,
But turns out, I'm quite the clumsy bane.
I trip on a shell and do a big spin,
My friends laugh so hard, I forgot to grin!

Ice cream dribbled down my new shirt,
"Look, mom, I'm a living dessert!"
Seagulls dive-bomb, it's a feathery fight,
I swear they are plotting to steal my bite!

The Enchantment of Coastal Breezes

A breeze whispers secrets under the sun,
But my hat's off again, it's all in good fun.
Laughter erupts as it takes to the sky,
Chasing it wildly like I'm made to fly!

Flip-flops flop and find their own dance,
Each step is a giggle, a silly romance.
Watch out for waves with a sneaky splash,
Wet clothes and a grin, oh what a smash!

Moonlit Memories by the Tide

As the sun snoozes, silver waves play,
Old crabs parade in their stylish ballet.
We sit on the sand, sharing marshmallow tales,
While the wind tells secrets of night-time gales.

Footprints in the sand lead to nowhere at all,
A mix of giggles comes with the night's call.
With fireflies dancing, we're lost in the haze,
In the end, it's just fun that brightens our days!

Periwinkle Skies and Radiant Light

Seagulls squawk in a sunny display,
Wearing their shades like stars of the bay.
Flip-flops flying with every new dive,
As beach balls bounce, the fun comes alive.

Kids crying over a melting ice cone,
While crabs dance like they're in a sitcom.
Sunburned noses and laughter abound,
Every flip of a towel, fun's already found.

Patterns of Driftwood Dreams

Driftwood sculptures that look like a horse,
Or maybe a werewolf, oh, who's keeping course?
Sandcastles built with a bucket and grin,
Till waves steal the throne, let the chaos begin!

A sun hat flies off in a gusty wee breeze,
The bather's pursuit is as silly as these.
Sudden splashes and pratfalls galore,
With laughter that echoes, who could ask for more?

Cobalt Waves and Timeless Tales

Flip-flops stuck like barnacles on feet,
Who knew a walk could feel so complete?
Waves crash in rhythm to the tunes of the shore,
As we dance in the circle, craving encore!

A picnic blanket going rogue in the air,
Lunch left to fend for itself—oh, beware!
Seashells tell stories more wild than a plot,
In this sandy realm, all worries are forgot.

Radiance in the Wave's Embrace

Sandy toes spark joy in the summer sun,
While jellyfish glide, oh, that looks like fun!
A splash from a friend sends us both for a spin,
We vow next time, not to dive right in.

The sunscreen fight, oh, what a sight to see,
A slippery battle, lather your buddy!
With laughter unending, we bask and we play,
In this beachside tale that won't fade away.

Breezes of Warmth and Wonder

The seagulls squawk, they never hush,
As ice cream drips in a sticky rush.
Flip-flops slap with each silly stride,
Sunburned noses, let's take a ride!

The beach ball pops, what a grand scene,
Chasing our dreams like a kid's cuisine.
Sandcastles crumble, a great big flop,
Who needs a throne? I'm a sand king on top!

Tidal Echoes Under the Sun

Waves tickle toes, and shells sing sweet,
Crabs wave their claws, a crustacean greet.
Fellow beachgoers, in chaos they dance,
Catching a Frisbee, it's pure happenstance!

With sunscreen on, we're a sight to behold,
The beach looks like Picasso's bold.
Sandwiches fly in a gusty parade,
Ugly tan lines? A fashion upgrade!

Meditations on Endless Blue

Floating in circles like a silly duck,
My inflatable unicorn ran out of luck.
The sunhats fly like a flock of birds,
While sunscreen wars break out with no words.

Each wave brings laughter, a puddle of fun,
"Oh no! A wave!" then all of us run.
Beach games of skill, let's roll the dice,
Throwing my towel? Oh, that's so nice!

Elysium of Waves and Dunes

Kites soaring high against the clear sky,
While sandbar surfers like dolphins fly.
Pretzels and lemonade, oh what a pair,
Together they dance in this sun-kissed air!

Beach volleyball, we aim for the moon,
The ball lands in soup, oh what a tune!
Waves whisper secrets, I giggle and grin,
The best days of summer, let the fun begin!

Lullabies of Ocean and Sky

The gulls sing loud, a raucous sound,
While llamas in tutus prance around.
The seaweed wiggles, doing the twist,
A fish in a bowtie? Nope, can't resist!

Bubbles pop like silly balloons,
With crabs that dance to jazzy tunes.
A jellyfish floats, wearing a grin,
As beach balls orbit, let the fun begin!

The Poetry of Driftwood and Dune

A turtle in shades sips on a drink,
While sandcastles wobble, about to sink.
Seashells gossip, oh what a treat,
As seagulls pass notes for a summer feat.

The starfish are plotting a beachside show,
With clams as the chorus, oh don't you know?
The sun dos a flip, tan lines in tow,
Makes everyone giggle, put on a show!

Celestial Bonds of Tide and Shore

As waves chase each other, they play peek-a-boo,
While octopi juggle, oh what a view!
The sun wears shades, like a cool old dude,
And starfish are partying, full of good food.

Mermaids trade secrets with seahorses spry,
While crabs deal in rumors, oh my, oh my!
The horizon winks, it's a sight to see,
As coconuts fall, laughing with glee.

An Immersion in Warmth and Waves

Rubber ducks race, it's a splash-tastic scene,
While dolphins are teasing, good-natured and keen.
The waves roll in with a bubbly cheer,
While flip-flops throw parties, oh let's all steer!

Sand is a canvas for doodles and dreams,
As kids build tall towers, bursting at seams.
The ocean's a playground, so full of zest,
Where laughter and joy are the ultimate quest!

Tide's Embrace

The waves rolled in with a splat,
A crab stole my sandwich, imagine that!
I chased him down the sandy hill,
He winked at me, said, "I'm full, what a thrill!"

The seagulls stole my chips as well,
They cawed and danced, oh what a spell!
A beach day turned into a chase,
Such is life in this watery place!

A Canvas of Timeless Tranquility

My towel's a lounge, all floppy and wide,
It caught the wind, and then it decided
To fly like a kite, oh what a sight,
I yelled, "Come back!" but it took flight!

I tried to build a sandcastle tall,
But my bucket betrayed me, it wobbled and fall,
A fort of crumbs, is all that remained,
The tide rolled in, and my dreams were drained!

Sunlit Pathways Along the Coast

Walking barefoot, I spotted a fish,
It jumped and giggled, quite a strange wish,
I asked it, "Hey, what's the secret to fun?"
It splashed me right back, and then it did run!

I tripped on my flip-flop, my foot went a-splay,
Landed in seaweed, oh what a display!
A sea sloth chuckled, with glee in his eyes,
While I waved hello, covered in fries!

Woven with the Sea's Breath

A wave crashed down, it stole my hat,
A dolphin wore it, imagine that!
We laughed and played, the tide was grand,
I thought I'd sunbathe, but now I'm in sand.

The sun shone bright like a playful prank,
My drink tipped over, oh how it drank!
The ocean's laughter echoed anew,
As I yelled, "Life's a beach, and I'm the fool too!"

Reflections on Sunlit Waters

Seagulls laugh as they dive and swoop,
Belly flops land like a big, loud whoop.
Kids build castles with moats so grand,
While parents search for their lost flip-flop band.

Crabs in a hurry hurry across the sand,
I swear they're plotting to take over the land.
Umbrellas fly like kites in the breeze,
Sunburnt noses bring humor to knees.

Beach balls bounce with a cheerful thud,
Someone joins in with a peanut butter flood.
The waves clap back like an audience clap,
In this seaside circus, who needs a map?

Ice cream drips faster than you can blink,
Melting dreams in every flavor you think.
Laughter rings out, a joyous parade,
In the sun's warm glow, where memories are made.

A Serenade in Aquamarine

A fish swims by with a goofy grin,
Waves tickle toes like a playful pin.
Sandcastles wobble with every new tide,
While hermit crabs make a comical slide.

Sunbathers lounge with hats that are wide,
As sunscreen smells waft and giggles collide.
Seashells gather stories, a secretive crew,
Whispering tales of things they once knew.

The beach ball's bounce has a mind of its own,
Whenever you reach it, it's suddenly flown.
Umbrellas are tilting, swaying like dancers,
Chasing lost toys like wild romancers.

Finally, the tide claims its sleepy throne,
As snacks and laughter begin to be sown.
With sunsets that blush like a cheeky grin,
The day's funny tales swirl like waves in a spin.

The Color of Tranquil Shores

Footprints zigzag like a mixed-up maze,
While ice cream cones melt in the sun's warm rays.
A dog plays fetch, determined and spry,
While a child yells, 'Hey! Look, I can fly!'

Beach towels flare like colorful flags,
While parents nap and the toddler drags.
Sandy sandwiches taste quite the same,
Who knew that grit could play such a game?

Flip-flops are squeaking like a couple of fools,
Rolling in laughter, not respecting the rules.
Goggles on faces, like aliens they gawk,
Buoyant and giggly around the beach walk.

Sunset paints skies in giggly hues,
As laughter and whispers drift on the bruise.
In this playful domain where fun never stops,
Tomorrow's another day to flaunt your flop-flops.

Sun-Drenched Echoes

The sun sings loud in a joyful trance,
While seagulls join in a wobbly dance.
Waves tickle toes as they rush and play,
Collecting wet shells at the end of the day.

A crab scuttles by in a balletic prance,
While sunscreen fights off the rays in a stance.
Life guards stand tall like fashion models,
Watching over waves with their cool, clammy coddles.

Sun hats wobble in the gentle wind,
As ice cream drips down, like a sweet, creamy sin.
Children shout, "Look! I'm a dolphin today!"
While kites in the sky would really like to stay.

As dusk rolls in, with a glimmering grin,
The funny echoes of laughter begin.
With blankets all laid, the stars start to wink,
In this magical place, who needs to think?

The Palate of the Sea

A clam jumped up to say, 'Hey there!'
'Forget the fish, let's grab a chair!'
The shrimp declared, with great bravado,
'I've had enough of this salty shadow.'

A lobster danced, a sight to see,
Wearing shades and sipping a sweet tea.
The seagulls laughed, took to the skies,
'Next year, we'll host the grandest fries!'

The wave splashed back, oh what a tease,
It whispered, 'Come dance, if you please!'
And the crabs all crawled, in fancy shoes,
'It's a shell-tastic bash, who wants to choose?'

The tide rolled in, with a splash and bounce,
'On this beach, who needs to pounce?'
With jokes and jests, they claimed their land,
For every wave, there's laughter planned.

Dreams Cast in Brilliance

A fish in a tux, what a sight!
Claiming the waves, by morning light.
'The sea's my stage,' he said with flair,
'Watch me wiggle, all without a care!'

Starfish were judges, sitting in rows,
'With legs like those, he'll steal the shows!'
A dolphin chimed in, 'Let's bring the band!'
And the sea turtles brought the conch shell brand.

The octopus played the tambourine,
Eight arms dancing, oh what a scene!
Everyone cheered for this reef soirée,
Who's next on stage? We can't delay!

So beneath the sun, with bubbles and jest,
The ocean's humor surely knows best.
It's a canvas of joy, every tide brings cheer,
With dreams in the waves, let's all volunteer!

A Tapestry of Sand and Sea

A crab wore a hat, crooked and bright,
Said, 'I rule this patch, from day to night!'
The seagull squawked, 'That's quite a dream!'
'Let's compete for the best team!'

They built up castles, quite a sight,
With moats of salt, polished all night.
The tide came in, they started to sweat,
'Next year, I'll build one I won't regret!'

Then a snail chimed in, moving so slow,
'I'll challenge you all, just watch me go!'
With a wink and a nod, he drew up a plan,
A race of the critters, oh, what a jam!

So they rolled and they giggled, until it was late,
Under moonlit skies, they celebrated fate.
In this land of laughter, so wild and free,
No winner too serious, all happy to be!

Cerulean Visions

In the deep blue, a whale took flight,
Said, 'I'm too big to hide from the light!'
With a splash and a flip, he made a big scene,
'The ocean is my stage, it's fit for a queen!'

The jellyfish glowed, a party of sorts,
Twinkling like stars, in swirling cohorts.
They danced through the night, with style and flair,
'Join us, dear fish, and shed your despair!'

Octopus served snacks, a gourmet display,
'With fresh ocean fries, we'll party all day!'
The sea urchins bobbed, enjoying the beat,
With spikes in the air, they couldn't be beat!

So they laughed and they twirled, with no care to show,
A silly parade, in the aquamarine flow.
In this whimsical world, where fish all convene,
Dreams take to the waves, where everything's seen!

Serenity Beneath the Azure Sky

A crab in a tux, looking so neat,
Dances on waves with swift little feet.
The sun spills laughter, warms the sand,
As seagulls practice their rock 'n' roll band.

Flip-flops flying, a race with the tide,
Who knew the ocean was such a wild ride?
A sunburned nose, a bright pink surprise,
While kids chase the waves, full of giggles and cries.

Beach balls are bouncing, sails can't stay straight,
The ocean's a jester, it's really first-rate.
Picnics are scattered, ants play the part,
As sandcastles tumble—oh, the ocean's such art!

With each wave that crashes, a splash of delight,
We'll dance on the shore till the fall of the night.
Laughter echoes, time slips right away,
In silliness reigns, we'll forever stay.

The Lure of Shimmering Dunes

A parrot named Paul, he knows how to chat,
Spouts funny lines, while wearing a hat.
The sand's like a blanket, warm and inviting,
But sometimes it feels like the sun is just biting.

With shovels and buckets, they build in the heat,
A fortress of sand, and what's that? A seat?
The tide comes a-calling, "Let's join in the fun!"
But little Timmy's stuck, oh, what have we done?

A picnic of sandwiches, chips in a pile,
Ants crash the party with a mischievous smile.
With lemonade spills, and laughter out loud,
Even the crabs are hoisting a crowd.

Jellyfish jiggle, they slip and they slide,
While the wise old beach ball just rolls with the tide.
At dusk we all gather, the sun takes a bow,
Thank goodness for laughter, we're silly, and how!

Echoes of a Seaglass Symphony

A shell serenade as waves chase the shore,
And turtles in tutus join in for some more.
The sand's like confetti from a grand parade,
While jellyfish waltz, not a moment delayed.

With boogie boards flying, they battle the sea,
"Look at me! Look at me!" calls out little Lee.
But alas, there's a splash, and his grin disappears,
As the big wave approaches, all laughter and cheers.

A beach ball collision sends everyone running,
With giggles and shrieks, oh, isn't it stunning?
In flip-flops they scamper, over sandcastles tall,
The ocean's a riddle, we're all in its thrall.

As shadows grow long and the sun dips away,
We wave to the sky, we've had quite a day.
With memories gathered and laughter in tow,
We dance to the rhythm of the water below.

Horizons Paint the Twilight

The sun's golden cheeks blush at day's end,
While dolphins perform, they just love to blend.
A kite's in the air, caught in a swirl,
As kids do the crab while giving a twirl.

The sand's now a stage where seagulls take flight,
While beach-goers laugh at this comical sight.
The ice cream melts quickly, it rolls from the cone,
And sticky fingers wave as they gnaw on a bone.

A treasure hunt starts; oh, what will they find?
Just seashells and sand, and a very lost mind.
The day softly whispers, we'll do this again,
For adventure and joy are like waves—without end.

The twilight's a canvas, a colorful show,
As we gather our treasures from the days we outgrow.
With stars peeking in, a giggle takes flight,
As we dream of the fun, from morning till night.

Resplendent Coastlines

The crab in the sun wears a hat so fine,
Dancing on beaches, he sips on brine.
Seagulls squawk tales of treasure and woe,
While swimmers lose trunks in a breeze they don't know.

Umbrellas like mushrooms sprout all around,
With kids making castles that soon tumble down.
A dog steals a sandwich, runs off with a cheer,
Sandwiches fly—now that's some beach flair!

Sunburned and laughing, the folks hit the waves,
But out comes a dolphin, it seems he misbehaves.
He flips with a splash, they squeal and they shout,
As water becomes a circus, no doubt!

With every sunsetting, the stories unfold,
Of mischief and giggles, and laughter retold.
In the twilight's dim glow, they sip on some soda,
While raccoons plot antics, they're sure they're a quota.

The Allure of Pelagic Enchantment

A fish in a tux sings, 'Come dance on the reef!'
His fins are quite fancy, beyond belief.
The octopus winks with a sly, knowing grin,
As clam parties start with a shell-swirled spin.

Mermaids burst out laughing, they spy on the shore,
While sailors drop anchors, then drop them some more.
'Yo ho!' says a pirate, all covered in sand,
His parrot is squawking, 'You should wash that hand!'

A crab throws a party with seaweed confetti,
And all of the starfish say, 'Isn't this petty?'
They dance in a circle, all happy and bold,
As stories of folly and friendship unfold.

A whale crashes in with a splash so grand,
Making waves that propel the whole beach from the land.

They laugh and they cheer, life's simpler here,
In waters enchanting, where joy has no fear.

Mosaic of Light on Water

The sun bakes pies in the sky overhead,
While jellyfish jiggle, and snails want to tread.
Crabs play chess with each other on rocks,
And call it a match for their dinner-time stocks.

Flip-flops go flying, a toddler's delight,
As seagulls swoop down, they claim their flight.
Each splash from a wave gets a giggle or shout,
While a beach ball rolls on, there's no escaping doubt!

Turtles race slowly, yet think they're so fast,
While children all cheer, their toes in the cast.
The day winds to dusk with a shimmering glow,
As laughter and joy in the currents flow.

A crab in a bowtie shakes hands with a seal,
Making plans for tonight—for a seafood meal!
Under the moonlight, with treasures in sight,
They toast to the ocean, what a fun night!

Enchanted Shores of Warmth

The sun loungers laugh and spill drinks everywhere,
As someone's lost flip-flop is caught in the air.
A toddler in floats chases waves with delight,
While parents with sunburns plot their next flight.

Sandcastles rise high only to face the tide,
While mermaids in sarongs make a stylish slide.
The seagulls engage in a food theft spree,
And tourists just chuckle, 'Is that fish for me?'

Surfboards stand proud as they try to align,
But one brave old surfer just hopes he won't twine.
With cheeky waves crashing, it's all in good jest,
As laughter rolls like the ocean—a real zest!

With marshmallows roasting on sticks by the shore,
S'mores stolen by raccoons, it's never a bore.
As day fades to night, laughter echoes like charms,
In a world drenched in joy, and a love that warms.

The Lullaby of the Marine Whisper

In the breeze where the seagulls parade,
A crab wears a hat, oh what a charade!
Fish tell tall tales as they swim by,
Laughing at mermaids who forget how to fly.

The starfish is grumpy, his friends are away,
Wishing the tide would come out to play.
A dolphin's cartwheel sends everyone spinning,
While clams gossip loudly, pretending to sing.

Shells gather round for a monthly debate,
On who has the finest, and who's going straight.
Coral reefs chuckle, in colors so bright,
As waves check their hair in the warm morning light.

With a wink and a splash, the ocean's alive,
Where jellyfish dance, and the sea cucumbers jive.
Close your eyes, feel the rhythm and cheer,
For under the sea, there's laughter to hear.

Veils of Mist and Light

Beneath the mist, a boat does a lurch,
With a captain who swears he's found his own perch.
A fish with a bowtie sneaks past his side,
Chuckling at sailors who grin and then slide.

The fog rolls in thick, like grandma's old stew,
While pirates get lost, finding treasures for two.
They stumble and tumble, oh what a sight,
Trading tales with the gulls, well into the night.

A seal with a surfboard thinks he's so cool,
While crabs throw a party by the old coral pool.
The waves seem to giggle, in a splashy ballet,
As dolphins keep score in their playful display.

With laughter so loud that the shore starts to sway,
The coastline's a stage, come join the fun play!
For the mist is a veil, but the joy's out of sight,
In the heart of the ocean, everything feels right.

Under the Gaze of Diving Albatross

An albatross swoops, with a wink from above,
His friends all dive down, like a flock on the shove.
"Keep your head up!" he squawks, as they tumble and swirl,
Then nearly gets caught in a whirl of a pearl.

The octopus winks in a game of charades,
While collecting some shells in his multi-colored braids.
A shrimp cracks a joke that makes everyone laugh,
As a crab plays his fiddle, giving them a good half.

The gulls start a rumble, each one takes a bet,
On which fish will swim right under the net.
But alas, they all bubble, and flip without care,
Making waves into giggles, all over the air.

Beneath the wide sky, life dances and spins,
With laughter and silliness that never thins.
So take off your worries, dip toes in the spray,
For under the albatross, friendship's the way!

The Treasure of the Shimmering Coast

The treasure is hidden, or so they all say,
But Captain McGiggles just laughs all the way.
With a map made of jelly, and crumbs from his cake,
He stumbles on rocks, makes a terrible quake.

Clams guard their bounty with a serious frown,
While tossing confetti like they're the town clown.
The mermaids are practicing their best belly flop,
As the waves cheer them on, never wanting to stop.

"Here's a map, here's a riddle!" yells a wily old seal,
With a treasure chest brimming with kelp for a meal.
"Gather round, folks, let's make it a game!
For who needs gold when the laughter's the flame?"

So join in the search, let your giggles take flight,
For the bounty of friendship is a sparkling delight.
With the sun setting low, and the tide rolling in,
The coast gives us treasures, where true fun begins.

The Ballad of the Beach

A crab in a hat danced on the shore,
With a flip and a flop, it wanted much more.
It sang to the seagulls, who rolled their eyes,
While beachgoers laughed at its silly surprise.

The sun baked us well, like bread in a pan,
We tried to build castles; they looked like a man.
But the tide came in quickly, our dreams washed away,
And the crab took a bow, as if in a play.

With sunscreen on noses, we sprawled on the ground,
Our laughter echoed, such joy to be found.
A seagull swooped down, stole fries from our plate,
It flew off, so smug, oh, it must feel so great!

When evening approached, we packed up our gear,
A sunburnt parade; we waved with good cheer.
Tomorrow we'll return, the beach calls our name,
To repeat all the fun in this silly game.

Embraced by the Ocean's Gift

At dawn, I found seashells, all glitter and gleam,
They whispered sweet secrets, or so it would seem.
One joked of a mermaid, with hair made of foam,
Yet claimed she preferred her warm, sandy home!

The waves rolled in laughter, the tides danced around,
While a starfish named Gary played tag on the ground.
He slipped on a seaweed; oh, what a big splash!
He laughed as he floated and made such a dash!

Seagulls were squawking, a raucous brigade,
Discussing their plans for a fishy charade.
They'd swoop and dive down; it was quite a display,
While beachgoers gawked at their comical play.

As night fell like dipped ice cream on our heads,
We danced on the shore, leaving footprints like threads.
Tomorrow we'll come back, to laugh and to play,
By the water's edge, in the sun's warm ballet.

Marigold Dreams and Cerulean Whispers

With buckets and shovels, we built a grand fort,
While a tiny blue crab made itself quite the sport.
It critiqued our work with an eye for design,
And promptly knocked over our towers, so fine!

A seagull swooped down, a mischievous sprite,
It snatched my sandwich; oh, what a flight!
I waved my arms wildly, but it just squawked back,
And then it sat laughing, my lunch in its pack!

The sun glinted brightly; the sand was so hot,
We played "Dodge the Puddle"—guess who got caught?
With giggles erupting, we splashed like the sea,
But our fun took a turn—bikini went free!

As sunset embraced us in shades of soft gold,
We danced by the shore, stories playful and bold.
Tomorrow we'll return, our toes in the grit,
With crabs as our playlist and seagulls to fit!

Starlight on Silken Waves

The beach at night was a curious sight,
With jellyfish glowing, a whimsical light.
They bobbed like balloons, all dressed up to tease,
While a lazy old dog snoozed by the breeze.

The stars twinkled laughter, shining up high,
As fish played peek-a-boo, oh my, oh my!
We built silly dreams with sandcastles grand,
Till the tide rolled in fast; they just floated and fanned.

In the moon's silver glow, we stumbled and tripped,
And laughed till we cried at the way that we skipped.
A shadowy figure emerged just ahead,
'Twas a raccoon with our snacks, but he fled like the wind!

So we toasted our drinks, to the night and the fun,
With gummy fish treats; our laughter begun.
Tomorrow, we'll return for more seaside cheer,
With jellyfish jams for all to hear!

An Ocean of Honeyed Glow

A donut fell from the sky, oh my!
It laughed as it rolled, brought joy to a pie.
Seagulls cried, 'What a treat!' as they tried,
To catch sugary waves, where jellies abide.

And then came a crab, with a rainbow pin,
Dancing in circles, with a cheeky grin.
He flipped through the foam, while we all cheered,
For a crustaceous jig that we all revered.

A dolphin in shades, sparkled so bright,
Told jokes about fish as it leapt in delight.
"I once saw a shark!" it said with a wink,
"Wearing a tutu and sipping a drink!"

With laughter that echoed, we splashed some more,
As cupcake waves crashed upon the shore.
With giggles and silliness, the sun started to set,
We left with our memories, the best kind yet!

Cobalt Shores of Delight

In a flip-flop race, we gathered the crew,
Losing the contest but soaking in dew.
Sandcastles crumbled at a sneeze or a cough,
As we built mighty towers, just to knock them off.

A turtle so slow, wore sunglasses with flair,
Trying to dance but went nowhere, I swear!
With every wild twist, he tripped on his shell,
The whole beach erupted, oh boy, what a sell!

Seaweed would tickle our toes as we shrieked,
Playing hide and seek with a crab that we peaked.
He mocked us with claws, gave a waving salute,
While seagulls staged laughter, in their own little boot.

As waves rolled in, we gathered at dusk,
With sand in our hair and a scent of sweet musk.
We danced under stars, as the tide pulled us near,
In this place of pure joy, we forgot all our fear!

Serendipity Under the Waves

A fish in a bowtie swam by with a glide,
Said, "Welcome to my party, come on, let's ride!"
With bubbles that danced, and sea urchins that pranced,
We laughed through the currents, entranced as we chanced.

At the bottom of blue, we found treasure galore,
A chest full of snacks, but no gold, we implore!
With nachos and salsa, we feasted like kings,
While jellyfish floated in their whimsical swings.

A pirate with parrot sang songs of delight,
Claiming all fish were dancing that night.
With each wave that tickled, we rocked with the tide,
While sea cucumbers tried to dance, full of pride.

Back on the shore, the laughter rang loud,
As crabs joined our games, oh how we felt proud.
A day full of whimsy, we floated away,
Under whimsical seas, where we love to sway!

The Glistening Mirage

On a surfboard made of marshmallow cream,
I rode on a wave, like a sweet dream.
With gummy bears cheering, it was quite a sight,
While flip-flops flew high, in the warm sunlight.

We found a parade of rubber ducks,
As they floated by, giving us clucks.
With every squawk, a new joke would appear,
Creating a fest of giggles and cheer.

As the sun began dipping, it turned quite absurd,
A sandcastle family had spread the word.
With tiny flags waving, they started a dance,
I joined in their jig, taken by chance!

So under a sky painted pink with glee,
We feasted with laughter by the deep blue sea.
With sloshing and splashing, and smiles all around,
In a mirage of joy, we forever were bound!

Diaphanous Dreams on Coastal Winds

In a hammock we sway, oh so wide,
A seagull steals our snacks, with great pride.
Every wave that crashes, a wacky sound,
Our thoughts are lost somewhere, never found.

Sunburned noses, a sight so grand,
In our flip-flops, we take a stand.
Laughter echoes, beach ball in tow,
Feet in the water, we're a goofy show.

Sand grains like treasures, we sift through,
The ice cream melts faster than our crew.
Tidal pull brings the giggles, too,
We're splashing around, just me and you.

Underneath the sun, we plot our schemes,
Building castles that topple like dreams.
Life's a beach, or so we say,
With sand in our snacks, we'll play all day.

The Luster of Distant Horizons

Chasing crabs, they're fast as a jet,
But we're too slow, so we place our bet!
With buckets in hand, we look for pearls,
Only to find our lunch—what a whirl!

Bright umbrellas lean, as if taking a nap,
While laughter erupts from a jumping chap.
We dive for shells like we're on a quest,
Who knew shoreline fun could be so blessed?

Floppy hats fly with each wild breeze,
We all chase after, "Oh, spare some cheese!"
Our beach ball's decided to roam and run,
Turning beach volleyball into quite the fun.

As sunset comes glimmering on the sea,
We stomp around like it's a jubilee.
Collecting memories, our hearts are bright,
In this endless joy, we'll dance till night.

Emotions Carried by the Current

Waves roll in, tickling our toes,
But watch out for jellys—oh, the woes!
Our laughter's loud, it competes with the tide,
As we hold our breaths, and brace for the ride.

Surfboards everywhere, it's a circus of fun,
While penguin waddles make the day run.
With sunscreen splats like abstract art,
Our worst moments steal the best part.

Sandy sandwiches, both crunchy and wet,
And sandcastle dreams now a tangled mess yet.
With quirky sunburns, we're a sight to see,
In swimsuits that don't quite fit, oh me!

Dunked in water, our giggles take flight,
Who knew a wave could bring such delight?
With each splash and a slip, we just laugh and shout,
Life on the shore is what it's about!

The Mirage of Sunlight and Seafoam

Campfire stories, with marshmallows near,
We roast the night, fueled by our cheer.
The stars wink down, like some fancy show,
As the water reflects, we let our thoughts flow.

A trek to the five-star, well, ice cream stand,
We spill our treats—what a sticky hand!
But grins abound, as we dig in deep,
Oh, the joys of summer, they'll never sleep!

Paddle boards glide, like penguins afloat,
In our borrowed boat, we try not to gloat.
Each little splash, a giggle released,
As we plot our grand adventures, at least!

Morning sun rises; it's a circus we spun,
With flip-flops jiving, we're not quite done.
So here's to the quirks of our seaside spree,
In this goofy haven, we'll always agree.

Lighthouses Calling in the Distance

Seagulls squawk like they own the place,
While I chase crabs at a comical pace.
My flip-flops flop, I stumble and trip,
A dance with the waves, oh what a slip!

The lighthouse winks, its light's a wild tease,
Beacons of nonsense, they bring me to knees.
I yell a hello, the ocean just laughs,
It splashes my face and steals my sun baths!

Sandcastles tumble in a gusty embrace,
With moats that resemble a watery race.
The tide's my nemesis, a cheeky old friend,
With every wave crash, my plans it will bend!

Twirling in circles, I lose track of time,
While jellyfish frolic, all slippery rhyme.
They jiggle and wiggle, the seaweed is sly,
In this wacky world, oh me, oh my!

Whispers of Sunlit Shores

Dear sun, don't burn me, I beg for a tan,
While dodging the sunscreen, it's part of the plan.
My beach chair collapses, oh what a delight,
A game of quick fixes, all through the night!

The surfboards are giggling, catching my eye,
As I wobble and tumble, I know I can't fly.
A seagull swoops down, it steals my last fry,
In this grand ocean tale, oh me, oh my!

Shells whisper secrets, the crabs play charades,
With legs like they've danced through the endless parades.

A dolphin pops up, wearing shades just for fun,
I tip my hat; he's the beach's number one!

The sun wants to chat, but I'm here for the fun,
With laughter and splashes, till the day is done.
So here's to the shenanigans, ocean-side cheer,
With whimsical whispers that make my heart steer!

Tides of Amber Dreams

On the shore, I spot a peculiar sight,
A flip-flop parade, oh what a delight!
They dance through the bubbles in their own crazy way,
While I laugh at their antics, this bubbly ballet!

The tide rolls in softly, with giggling waves,
As my ice cream drips down; I swear it misbehaves.
Seashells applaud; the afternoon's fun,
An amber sun setting, the day nearly done!

Children's laughter echoes, a symphony free,
While I search for treasures, or maybe just me.
With buckets and shovels, a squad of delight,
In this realm of sandcastles, we'll dance till the night!

Curious crabs join our jubilant crew,
They wiggle and scuttle, like they've nothing to do.
In the tides of my dreams, I find spirits of glee,
With waves full of laughter, it's all meant to be!

Azure Embrace

In a sea of blue, I try to hold on,
A beach ball is bouncing; oh boy, it's gone!
My friends all keep laughing, as I chase the orb,
What a silly race, it's my summer absorb!

Floating on noodles, we sip from our cups,
As the world spins around, with silly hiccups.
They say I'm a mermaid; I swim like a fish,
But I'm more like a dolphin; a flopping-fish wish!

Shells line the shore like the stars in the sky,
Each whisper of waves gives a wink to the shy.
With sunscreen as armor, I'm ready for thrills,
In this comedy ocean, I'm conquering spills!

As the sun starts to dip, we chat and we cheer,
With stories of mischief that ring through the year.
In this azure embrace, laughter takes flight,
Under the glow of the moon, everything's bright!

Kisses from the Salty Breeze

The seagull stole my picnic treat,
I chased it down with quickened feet.
It laughed and soared with great delight,
As I fell sand-first, what a sight!

The waves are laughing, can't you hear?
They tickle toes, they spread good cheer.
My flip-flops flew, now where'd they go?
A mystery only the tides know!

I built a castle, tall and grand,
With a moat around, oh isn't it grand?
But a wave rolled in with a cheeky grin,
Now I just boast of where it had been!

The sunset whispers, "Don't be shy,
Let's splash around, give it a try!"
With each big splash, we dance and tease,
The salty kiss, how sweet it is!

A Tapestry of Radiant Shores

I brought my towel, bright and bold,
The sun, it mocks, now I feel cold.
With legs like jelly, I take the sand,
Imitating a crab, it wasn't planned!

A sandcastle stood, proud and high,
Until a kid yelled, "Let's make it fly!"
With a flying leap, and a mighty crash,
My masterpiece met its savage splash!

Shells collected, treasures galore,
But my bucket got stuck in the door.
I stood with laughter, oh what a sight,
The wind, it took my hat in flight!

As dusk approaches, I see the glow,
My friends all gather, putting on a show.
The sandy dance, we jump and sway,
Inviting the stars to join our play!

The Call of the Tranquil Sea

The ocean calls, or is it my phone?
I dropped it in a wave, my own!
With sand in my hair, I hear it beep,
But the fish are laughing, I take a leap!

A beach ball bounced like a silly jest,
My poor sunblock just didn't rest.
As it flew away in a joyous spree,
I swore it might be gaining a degree!

The sun is setting, the sky's ablaze,
But I just tripped; it's one of those days.
A toe in the water, oh what a mix,
Now the jellyfish thinks it's time for tricks!

With laughter echoing through the night,
We dance like seagulls, what a sight!
We're on a quest for snacks, oh yes!
Each bite, a memory, we confess!

Reflections in the Aquamarine

The ocean shimmers, a mirror so bright,
I checked my hair, oh what a fright!
With seashell earrings and a hat so wide,
I thought it chic, but oh, I lied!

A crab took notice, gave me a stare,
With claws held high, he didn't care.
He strutted by, like a tiny king,
I laughed so hard, I dropped my ring!

The tides roll high, then tumble down,
My inner mermaid, now lost in town.
I tried to swim, but the waves just giggled,
As my mask and snorkel nearly just wiggled!

With friends around, we share our cheer,
Making waves, spreading no fear.
Let's paint the night with our silly tales,
Under the stars, our laughter sails!

Secrets of the Shoreline

Crabs in shells do the crabby dance,
While seagulls plot a fishy romance.
Flip-flops squawk as they hit the ground,
Crazy seashells are what we've found.

A sunburned tourist takes a stride,
He trips on a wave with no place to hide.
With sunscreen smeared all over his face,
He walks like a penguin in a frantic chase.

Sandcastles crumble underfoot's might,
While beach balls bounce out of sheer delight.
Sand in the sandwiches, a crunchy treat,
We munch on laughter, who needs to eat?

In the distance, a dolphin wears shades,
Winking at all in the fun-filled parades.
The shoreline's secret - it's totally wack,
Where giggles abound, and no one looks back.

Harmony in the Surf

The waves sing out a bubbly tune,
As surfers ride them on a cartoon.
With a splash and a laugh, they belly flop,
Underneath the sun, they twist and bop.

A seal gives a wink, quite the charmer,
As beachgoers chase, yelling 'bring the armor!'
Sideways coolers roll down the sand,
Where snacks and giggles are always on hand.

Kites zigzag high like they own the place,
While sandbars hide in the ocean's embrace.
Someone's lost their hat, it's flying free,
A seagull's new hat, oh what a spree!

Dancing jellyfish sway to the beat,
While flip-flops become the trendiest feet.
In the surf's embrace, joy is a fact,
Not a single sad face, it's more like a pact.

A Journey Through Sapphire Depths

Adventurers dive with snacks in tow,
Underneath the waves where wild things flow.
Fish with sunglasses swim past with glee,
While octopuses hide for a cheesy selfie.

Discovery calls from the depths below,
But first, let's savor a snack on the go.
Gummy fish and seaweed chips galore,
Laughing as we munch by the ocean floor.

Treasure maps sketched on napkins bright,
X marks the spot, oh what a sight!
Turns out it's just a crab with a shell,
He waves and shimmies, we can't help but yell!

The reefs buzz soft with a comic tone,
As turtles float past in relaxed zones.
We might just stay here, lost in our quest,
Emerging from laughter, we feel so blessed.

Threads of Sand and Sea

Tangled up in a towel with flair,
We find seashells hiding everywhere.
Matching flip-flops, one's gone astray,
As we chase the tide, come what may.

The sand seeks to stick, it's crafty in play,
While sunscreen sprays go wildly away.
Bikini tops flapping like flags in the breeze,
While laughter erupts as we aim for the tease.

Brave little kids build a moat with pride,
But hope it won't wash away with the tide.
As dads dive in for a wave like a champ,
They emerge like a seal, looking quite damp.

With every splash, comes a giggling cheer,
The ocean whispers fun, always near.
So here's to the coast, with humor so sweet,
Where every moment is a funny little treat!

Whispers of Sunlit Shores

Seagulls gossip like old friends,
While crabs perform their salsa bends.
A beach ball flies with noble flair,
And sunscreen smears make quite the pair.

Umbrellas dance in the coastal breeze,
As shoes disappear 'neath sand's tease.
Children laugh while kites take flight,
Building castles, oh what a sight!

Frisbees soar with epic grace,
Laughter echoes, a happy place.
Picnics spread with sandwich glee,
Ants arrive for the jubilee!

Sunburned noses, a classic view,
Ice cream drips, what to do?
We'll laugh it off, like summer cheer,
For those mishaps, we'll shed a tear!

Tides of Celestial Dreams

A crab wearing shades struts by the door,
While waves whisper secrets, oh so galore.
Starfish pose, unaware of their fame,
The ocean's a stage, a wild game!

Flipping burgers with seaweed flair,
Surfboards whisper, 'Life's only fair!'
A dolphin jumps through a hula hoop,
As seagulls cheer, forming a troop.

Tide pools filled with curious sights,
Shells proclaiming their ocean rights.
Jellyfish dance with such delight,
While sunburned folks look out of sight!

Wet towels flutter like flags at dawn,
Shimmery seashells, dreams that are drawn.
In chaos we laugh, a joyful scheme,
As waves crash on with a gentle beam!

Embrace of the Endless Horizon

A sea turtle in shades sips on a drink,
While jellybeans float, don't you think?
Fishermen nap as their lines untangle,
While seagulls steal fries in a risk they dangle.

Waves shout out 'Hey!' in joyful tones,
While beachcombers hunt for shiny stones.
Mermaids giggle, brushing their hair,
As surfboards tumble without a care.

Hats fly off in the playful wind,
Each tumble and toss, nature's good friend.
Sandwiches vanish, you take a bite,
Oops! There's mustard, what a sight!

With toes in water, life feels so grand,
Laughing at seagulls who raid the sand.
So here's to fun under the sun's gleam,
Life's a beach, or so it would seem!

A Dance with the Crystal Waves

Paddleboards wobble, a dance of sorts,
While llamas in swimsuits take to the courts.
Seaweed wigs worn with comic flair,
As beach chairs cling to the sun's warm glare.

The sun-cooked burgers roll in delight,
While salty air fills up the night.
With sunscreen wars and beach ball fights,
Who knew fun could reach such heights?

Seashell trumpets make quite a sound,
As laughter and joy float all around.
In flip-flops, we trip but never fall,
The ocean's embrace welcomes us all.

So let's dance like no one's watching,
With splashes and smiles, our hearts are catching.
With each wave calling us to explore,
Let's laugh our way back to the shore!

Waves of Gilded Serenity

On a stretch of glittering bliss,
Where seagulls argue and kids just miss,
The sand's a bit sticky, the sun's way too hot,
But there's always a drink in the cooler spot.

With flip-flops squeaking, we shuffle along,
A crab joins the conga, it can't go wrong,
Dancing with waves that splash and tease,
Laughing at sunburns, oh please, oh please!

We build castles with moats that never hold water,
While the tide decides it's their final slaughter,
"Look at my fortress, all regal and grand!"
Then splash! There goes my whole segmented land.

But amidst all the chaos, the laughter will soar,
With salty snacks served on our sandy floor,
We'll grin at the sun, our cheeks all ablaze,
As we plot our escape from reality's maze.

The Dance of Sun and Sea

Sunlight winks off a wave's slick back,
The beach ball rolls like it's on a track,
With everyone chasing that rogue little sphere,
Missteps and stumbles—oh dear, oh dear!

The wind takes a turn, my hat's in the air,
I duck and I dive like I just don't care,
The water's a shower, the waves quite the tease,
Oh, here comes a swoosh, I'm drenched to the knees!

A picnic's arranged on a checkered sheet,
But the seagulls swoop in, what a foul cheat!
With popcorn in beaks, they soar out of sight,
"Hey! That was my snack!" but they're up, what a flight!

Yet laughter erupts, we'll get even, it's true,
With crabby revenge we'll plot anew,
A day at the shore brings laughs without end,
As waves weave in stories that twist and bend.

Horizon's Luminous Embrace

With toes in the water and a grin ear to ear,
Why do I smell like a strange sea creature here?
My friend's giving orders, "Just dive, don't look back!"
But I'm flopping like flounder—oh, cut me some slack!

The sun turns us all into sizzling fries,
While sunscreen battles with sand, oh the cries!
"Did I miss a spot?" someone yells in despair,
Turns out, yes—they're a walking, burnt flare!

As kids skip by with buckets of dreams,
I step on a jellyfish, or so it seems,
With squeals that echo up to the sky,
I'll trade my lost flip-flop for a donut supply!

And as we all gather to watch the sun dip,
A friendly toast to the day's wild trip,
With laughter and tales, oh what a delight,
In the grand scheme of sand, we shine ever bright.

Shores of Sun-Kissed Memory

The sun's out here, shining like a star,
But my towel's stuck to me—oh, how bizarre!
Friends take me hostage, "Get in, just one splash!"
But I'm flailing like an octopus—oh, what a crash!

With kites soaring high and laughter all 'round,
A jellyfish wave left me tangled and wound,
"Did you see that?" I shout, pointing at glee,
But they're all busy avoiding my seaworthy spree!

Sandcastles rise up, so tall and so proud,
Till a rogue wave comes in, crashing their crowd,
"Mom! My castle!" the little ones scream,
But it's only a wave, not exactly a dream!

Yet nighttime brings stars glimmering bright,
With tales that's of laughter and coastal delight,
A toast to the moments that fell from the sky,
On shores where we'll always let our spirits fly.

A Symphony of Waves

The seagulls squawk a silly tune,
While crabs do a dance beneath the moon.
A beach ball hits a snoozing whale,
As kids run from a seaweed trail.

The tide rolls in with quite a splash,
And jellyfish float in a panicked dash.
A flip-flop flies, what a sight to see,
As dad trips over a sun-lotion spree.

Sandcastles rise with shaky grace,
While wind chimes play a song of haste.
A crab steals chips; what a tiny thief,
But parents just laugh, in disbelief.

So here we frolic, no worries in sight,
As waves giggle, feeling just right.
With sunscreen on our noses, bright pink,
We dive in the brine, give life a wink.

Essence of Radiant Shores

The sun's out here, a crispy fry,
As we try to sculpt a whale, oh my!
A sandcastle kingdom with moats and gates,
Till the tide rolls in, sealing their fates.

Oh silly gulls, they snack with flair,
Stealing fries right out of thin air.
But watch your toes; here comes a wave,
It's more like a hug, from the sea so brave.

Umbrellas flip like angry bees,
While sunscreen battles with sticky knees.
We laugh as a wave gives dad a shove,
He turns to the ocean; "Not what I love!"

Each wave a giggle, each splash a cheer,
On shimmering shores, we'll stay right here.
With sandy toes and salty grins,
Our adventure starts, let the fun begin!

Dunes Beneath the Sky's Caress

Dunes like castles stretch out far,
We race to the beach like a shiny car.
Frolicking kids and sunburnt toes,
While seagulls plot their fishy prose.

Buried in sand, a toy sword gleams,
While the ocean bubbles with silly dreams.
A wave sneezes, what a big splash,
And watches as us landlubbers clash.

Sandwiches fly like frisbees in flight,
As surfboards wobble into the night.
The sunscreen lather's a sticky affair,
But when we slip, it's laughter we share.

So let's build forts while the sun shines bright,
Swoosh through the waves, what a delight!
With each wild tumble and giggling cheer,
This sandy escapade is our favorite sphere.

Where the Sea Meets the Sun

Bikinis and shorts are quite the sight,
As we try to surf but end up in flight.
A wave appears, like a sneaky tease,
And splashes everyone with daring ease.

Flippered penguins keep trying to glide,
While beach balls bounce in an acrobatic ride.
Oh what a mix of joy and fright,
As sand gets tossed in a comical fight.

The ice cream melts faster than we can lick,
While flip-flops go missing, oh so quick.
Sand in our hair and on our cheeks,
Each hour here is a giggle that peeks.

With the sun setting low, we still go strong,
Singing fun songs, a joyful throng.
The ocean winks, giving us a nod,
As we frolic with glee, oh what a facade!

www.ingramcontent.com/pod-product-compliance
Lightning Source LLC
Chambersburg PA
CBHW072132070526
44585CB00016B/1642